Contents

Intro

During a ritual conducted around the statue of Harold Wilson outside Huddersfield station during *The Fourth World Congress of Psychogeography 2019*, participants were invited by Crab & Bee (Helen Billinghurst and Phil Smith) to make a promise to the future.

Mine was to 'actually write poems'.

This has happened, albeit during the lockdown period of the 2020 Covid-19 pandemic, which means the resulting writing was made in the context of an indoors-based existence. In this time physical walking was restricted to domestic living space, a small-scale geography opening out on to unwalkable distances comprising dream, memory, media and imagination.

Having decided to 'shield', both myself and my partner did not venture beyond the end of our garden path for some months, eventually 'easing' only to allow ourselves trips to collect prescriptions and walk to the postbox at the end of the road.

Not for us, then, the lockdown experiences of deep exploration of the locality, as the only places we were exploring were our own rooms – and on one occasion our roof when I cut down a fallen television aerial. Lack of aerial has done nothing to reduce our daily diet of TV however, the screen and its flow of images being a major element of the space we occupy. Screens of course not one-way as we are present to others (deliberately and otherwise) through various devices.

In a sense we perform being at home, with many aspects of performance such as costume, props, characters all clearly present. Larks against a background of death and fear.

During this time we are sustained by deliveries – itself a walking project as, although vehicles are involved in delivery, the deliverers walk considerable distances (16-18,000 steps per day in an article I read), a mass drift across driveways – paths – pavement – gardens.

As the lockdown proceeded this became for me a period of dreamy torpor punctuated with bursts of mental activity. My focus would float between concerns with practicalities ('What's the best way to get food delivered?'), theoretical questions ('Does poetry written as psychogeography have distinctive features?'), and fictions ('How are Sexton Blake and Mlle Yvonne going to escape from Dr Huxton Rymer's boat?') – the strands sometimes merging (dreaming the viewpoint of a 150-year-old detective peering at supply chains, the networks morphing into a kind of terrible ever extending vortex, giving rise to vertiginous fear of scale.)

The domestic archaeology of decluttering would unearth long-lost objects, such as the James Bond car from which the title of this sequence comes (a sideways 60s jump from Harold Wilson.)

I experienced a painful nostalgia for past and future walks, yet persisted in 'Don't Walk' mode, purposeful ambulation limited to steps on an exercise device, psychogeography confined to a screen-based expedition.

Out of all this – the experience of lockdown, the memories, some dreams, an extended virtual walk – I made the poems that were promised to a future that has now arrived.

James Bond car 1965

JAMES BOND DRIVING * SECRET OPERATING
FEATURES * RETRACTABLE MACHINE GUNS
OPENING ROOF AND EJECTOR SEAT * REAR
BULLET SCREEN * TELESCOPIC OVER-RIDERS
SECRET INSTRUCTIONS

A gift promising
exciting trajectories
through the grown-up world

a man in a painted suit (forever fixed in driving seat)
able to deploy spring-powered assistance (via our giant fingers)

journey comes cocooned with streamlined defense
push one button for solitude
two for concealment
three for an empty road
shot through to resolution
tracking lines of forward momentum
towards the horizon of requirement
: a golden journey

the (r)ejected passenger flies
sacrificed to
a covenant with time:

everything always onwards

just ask the supersonic kingsize
concrete fascias of the sunlit
squares

ask strontium

ask the cheery print of the instant
packaging

ask atomic Stingray
navigating New Elizabethan oceans
bubbling with potential

bounded only
by the 4-minute horizon

the ejecter drives
onwards to a serious somewhere
the ejectee hurtles
in an unexpected
arc . . .

Don't Walk

headlines reporting a different
quality of dreaming
experienced by an immobile
population

a slow wade through
submerged streams of distraction

now could be the optimum time to have
comforting Lovecraft reimagined in friendly
terms – safer zombies – a
multiverse reboot calibrated for
nostalgia – an edgelands fan site

to suck down pleasing palliatives

to sink beneath piles of
sugar-dusted fun fur

to tuck in to fatbergs
clogging the entertainment conduits:

but the dream machine dreams dreams
beyond the sponsors' sightlines
story arcs collapse
revealing hidden vision

the screen assumes the predictive
power of weather-sensing seaweed
nailed to the wheeled hut of a sepia downland
shepherd – a workmanlike tool
for prophecy

flicking the channel blocks like tarot
cards
illuminating unfixed
locations

commenced a regime
a monastic marking of the Hours
using TV series as the objects of meditation:
9am walking the flying headquarters of *Mascot's Agglomerations of Shift*
2pm walking the curved corridors of *Stateroom Triad: The Nice Gentlewoman*
4pm walking the floating passageways of *Seance Pavilion* –
switching to films at weekends to vary the texture –
The Lot of the Riots trilogy; *The Hurricane Gantries* series;
all the *Stateroom Triad* films from *The Motorcycle Pierrot* to *NeoGene*

watch enough stories flowing
through screens and you come to know
some things:
bluish light fibrillating over twitching limbs
is bad news
spreading black veins across the temples
is bad news
eyes turned completely black:
the worst

new brighter beings get
captured – suspended
in gel – disassembled –
warehoused on the outskirts

and the second season wasn't so good but
you can buy a copy of her jacket

All Boundary Roads

I decided to 'walk' along every road named Boundary Road, partly as nostalgia for the first 'shopping street' remembered (pushed there in pram and more recently walked to hundreds of times since – they could scatter me there after death) – however this walk was a confinement version using googlemaps – stroking a touchpad rather than striding along – it being a case of any port in a storm in these situations – virus laws guidance and caution making this mass of streets temporarily inaccessible as a fabled Forbidden City / Lost World / Hidden Earth

daily trips
an approximate gazetteer conjured in pixels
creating the world's double – a bargain golem

this action a minor stream flowing backwards through the surveillance channels
transforming my peripheral cell into the panopticon's central observation tower

at first seemed like a pointless and pallid exercise – no way to pick up an object / smell the air / buy a pasty from Julie's Cafe – no presence in the space – no there becoming here then once again there as steps and breaths are made

but noted after a while that the images of streets traversed in this way persisted like a microdose of dreams – odd items retained from the silt of the restricted letterbox drift – twilight wall of lives in the quiet windows of low-rise flats – small triangles of wild land – cherry trees older than the houses – cowboy wagon wheel mounted on a terraced house sounding to forgotten frontiers – two dead Christmas trees outside a garage opposite a medical device factory – the way graveyards and disused gasometers make stretches of open sky – an invocation

detritus of the google vehicle process – sudden shifts – blurred trapezoids hover in the air – ghost map on each click – summer becomes autumn in a single step – graffiti appears and is erased – figures striding the end of the boundary – blur faced cyphers become my fellow walkers trapped in the past – pedestrian bilocation – all included in the process

figured out a way to do the field notes – locate each Boundary Road with its
postcode + write a line describing something seen there + search the digital
traces of the location and scrape some found text – thus let some language
emerge from this broken-sidelong view of the network

trying to imagine all these roads as one long
road flowing from north to south to the first
road I remembered
     – despite some having dead ends some being circular
     – assemblage cut-up and wormhole training coming in handy
     – one hell of a crazy road

logged 89 'Boundary Road' signs
each a two-word paradox
boundary : drawing a line of furthest limit : dividing the world in two
road : laying an open way : connecting to next things

Down Boundary

Boundaries are not safe; they occupy neither time nor space...they let things through.
Alan Garner, *Boneland* (2012) quoted in *Foregrounding the Psychology in Psychogeography*, Andrea Capstick (2019)

I did not walk along Boundary Road EH14
trees heavy with shade   inspiring people who have blazed

I did not walk along Boundary Road G73
palisade fencing bent into shimmering curves   a guide to making
representations

I did not walk along Boundary Road KA8
tarmac speckled white   similar businesses nearby: the lost world

I did not walk along Boundary Road CA2
fenced in overgrown triangle   enhancer-promoter interactions were detected
in this locus

I did not walk along Boundary Road TS1
shuttered red building and a steel bridge   disoriented terms used are ritual

I did not walk along Boundary Road TS6
bungalows scoping cricket pitches   subjects of the sun-descended king

I did not walk along Boundary Road YO16
wild poppies surrounding a junction box   mobile mast on komfort house

I did not walk along Boundary Road LA1
glimpsed from a roundabout through dusty shrubbery   arise virtual solutions

I did not walk along Boundary Road FY8
gull gliding under gray cloud   everything was better than perfect

I did not walk along Boundary Road PR2
ginger cat alongside a red wall   random inspection to see who has a bin would
identify households with out a bin

I did not walk along Boundary Road BB5
strips of parched grass   attack on the distribution question

I did not walk along Boundary Road WF13
profusion of flowers   life's too connected

I did not walk along Boundary Road DN33
strip of shaded sunbricks   interim disqualification

I did not walk along Boundary Road S2
wires radiate from pole   a special smell – metallic I suppose

I did not walk along Boundary Road SK8
satellite dish above Celtic crosses   given a carrier bag with a tin of corned
beef biscuits and a large block of chocolate

I did not walk along Boundary Road M27
man with two carrier bags angles the railway line   friendly closeout experts
can help you

I did not walk along Boundary Road M44
bisecting an egg-shaped mandala   designed to help you develop key skills

I did not walk along Boundary Road WA1o
shuttered closed-down pub   the fish have started growing again

I did not walk along Boundary Road L21
wire fence dropping under brambles   "walking in shoes": practical
approaches

I did not walk along Boundary Road L36
stone cherub behind a grille   hide this for me for a couple of days

I did not walk along Boundary Road CH62
leotards tied to demolition site fence   they say love knows no reason and no
boundaries

I did not walk along Boundary Road CH43
houses face trees then a graveyard faces trees   the moment is being treated as
unexplained

I did not walk along Boundary Road NG24
green fenced hospital   raise high the ancient gateways

I did not walk along Boundary Road PE33
rhomboid green   airfield ward

I did not walk along Boundary Road NR6
superstores under the sun   stations for outdoor processions

I did not walk along Boundary Road NR29
straight track dividing flat fields   giving unrepeated access

I did not walk along Boundary Road NR31
horses on a rotting shed   turn your passion into one of these

I did not walk along Boundary Road NR14
single track almost a holloway   functions at the discretion of the
administrator

I did not walk along Boundary Road IP26
petals on tarmac   you keep discovering new rooms

I did not walk along Boundary Road IP28
sunbricks under blossom   the sanctuary was damaged by fire

I did not walk along Boundary Road CB6
coloured bands on the playzone   plumes of acrid smoke

I did not walk along Boundary Road CM23
pigeon over dusty track   please stop – it's not the 90s anymore

I did not walk along Boundary Road AL1
slate shaded porches   peeling off to their respective billets

I did not walk along Boundary Road NN13
skeletal sign-frame left on a verge   given more stretching opportunities

I did not walk along Boundary Road B74
trees lean across the curtilage   you've smiled and laughed with me with a
chicken tikka pathia through my best times

I did not walk along Boundary Road WS9
newbuild shrubs still small   after us not dust

I did not walk along Boundary Road DE65
concrete hobby horse barriers   effect significance matrix

I did not walk along Boundary Road DE22
cemetery under ragged sky   infectious laugh

I did not walk along Boundary Road NG9
cascade of dark leaves   three roses will be laid on the coffin

I did not walk along Boundary Road NG2
steps down into dim woods   studies of cosmochemical organic syntheses

I did not walk along Boundary Road LE12
partially-buried membrane showing through   flexible with shifts and location

I did not walk along Boundary Road LE2
concrete wall with a wire top   energy academy stress site

I did not walk along Boundary Road LE17
stepped-down house line   finite staff to deliver

I did not walk along Boundary Road CV21
new fence facing old fence   get round there and take a look!

I did not walk along Boundary Road HP1o
phone box with a circus poster   dreams head office

I did not walk along Boundary Road SL9
child caught in mid-swing   record has a record administrator assigned

I did not walk along Boundary Road HA5
bicurrent tree forms   listening to you and assisting you

I did not walk along Boundary Road HA9
flat-roofed units enclose a car park   in the highest grade of quality

I did not walk along Boundary Road N2
perimeter arc   around one million interments

I did not walk along Boundary Road N22
frozen terrace curve   just over a year later I find myself totally consumed

I did not walk along Boundary Road N9
delaminating marine ply garage doors   no letter for a colony or foreign
country may exceed two feet in length

I did not walk along Boundary Road SS9
low garden walls step curve step and drop   city fibre update

I did not walk along Boundary Road RM14
cherry blossom profile   must hold active INDIVIDUAL affiliation

I did not walk along Boundary Road RM1
aluminium sheets gleaming through greenery   we cannot view your
neighbour-to-neighbour conversations

I did not walk along Boundary Road IG11
SEE YOU IN THE FUTURE wraps a brick corner   the entity status is active

I did not walk along Boundary Road E13
radiating ironwork   substantial expertise in identifying picturesque

I did not walk along Boundary Road E17
pollarded tree beside railway bridge   the presence of migrating tribespeople

I did not walk along Boundary Road NW8
stretched out copse estate   they're saying that each of the homes will be
named after YBAs

I did not walk along Boundary Road DA15
half-timbered end terraces   imaginative ways people have added their steps

I did not walk along Boundary Road SW19
iron SSSƨ on high end-wall   we speak your language!

I did not walk along Boundary Road TW15
residential trident kissing a pylon angle   white fox photography

I did not walk along Boundary Road SL6
white gate with no fence   recent pop up events

I did not walk along Boundary Road RG14
pattern-bond brickwork under the sun   one less job to worry about!

I did not walk along Boundary Road SN15
stone obelisk with a rock head   ordinary life project

I did not walk along Boundary Road BS36
waves of willow over stone   mr max showing engine downthrust

I did not walk along Boundary Road BS11
buddleia flanking jacking pipes   a body was discovered submerged

I did not walk along Boundary Road BS24
kerbless curtilage   hopefully won't scream

I did not walk along Boundary Road PL31
skyline white development   the town's framework states

I did not walk along Boundary Road PL2o
mossy shed roof   totally wired electrical installation specialists

I did not walk along Boundary Road TQ6
blue gate and blue door both open   a thriving junior section

I did not walk along Boundary Road BA22
a shaded green layer   the pair are looking to bring their own touch

I did not walk along Boundary Road BH1o
long angled pedestrian bridges   mystery surrounds future

I did not walk along Boundary Road SP1
new wall efflorescence   cleaning services is a business

I did not walk along Boundary Road BN11
flint inset panels   a spitfire has filled the skies

I did not walk along Boundary Road BN15
road surface growth lines   rehabilitation activity requirement

I did not walk along Boundary Road GU26
figures against burning white playground   running out of time

I did not walk along Boundary Road GU1o
long-line space between trees   informal pedestrian crossing points

I did not walk along Boundary Road GU14
high-hooped atrium   learners destined for the workplace

I did not walk along Boundary Road GU21
pale spring leaves facing yellow walls   these are our core technologies

I did not walk along Boundary Road SM5
diamonds in the gable   balance flexibility and strength

I did not walk along Boundary Road RH1o
curved front steps   mix the generations project

I did not walk along Boundary Road RH17
curved line through woods   the old sense of wonder and refuge

I did not walk along Boundary Road TN2
surprise meadow and tangling hedge   a fountain of milk

I did not walk along Boundary Road ME4
powdery wooded distance   create a treasure basket

I did not walk along Boundary Road CT11
clock held on ironwork balcony   safety for the shipwrecked and health for the
sick

I did not walk along Boundary Road CT14
knotted ropes flank a garage   new signs between

I did not walk along Boundary Road CT21
crossbar flagpole in blue-fenced estate   urgent field safety notice

I did not walk along Boundary Road BN2
gasometers beyond a flint wall   gateway position

I did not walk along Boundary Road BN41
gingerbread trim gables over ice cream paintwork   the dividing line

Anti Nazi League march 1979

a sunny day

the route was planned to pass
a guesthouse known to welcome international
travellers in fascism
– Bormann-types after a seaside billet
and Thule Society holidaymakers

there was a fat man in shorts sitting
outside the breakfast-room bay windows
smirking at our parade of lollipop placards

signs offered VACANCIES
the ancient-always invite

Pilgrimage

dream: finding a map in a 70s-era paperback
pages loose and browned
a UK Camino
straight line diagrammatic routes
emanating from BRISTOL
one terminated in Galashiels

the day before the feeds were promoting
virtual pilgrimage challenges
YOU VS THE WORLD! GET
BLING! SEE YOU
ON STREETVIEW!
walk against the territory
along with placemarked pals: become landscape's adversaries
get hefty gleaming medals for Camino / Hadrian's Wall / Lands End

Moving On

obliged to carry the silk handkerchief
of a famous traitor
for passage through the unformed deep

finding a dry lion   a broken
water fountain set up for Jubilee
reasons jaw
now broken decades' slow spigot dribbling
forming a limescale trail down
to dusty grasses
on a curve of road with no pavement
and no debts forgiven

met a friend up by the Grenadier
he'd had a bit of bother but seemed
lively with his hair dyed orange excitedly saying
he had upgraded everything to PREMIUM

Hey, John!

a call came while I was cleaning the club one Sunday
morning, must have been 1985, it was John
the sound man
wanted me to get some of the previous night's takings
to pay his fines so he could get out of jail

what it was
he had a car business of sorts
various dead vehicles
left on the road accruing fines
which John argued were unfair
as the cars could not move
(some of them merely chassis with fewer
than four wheels)
really not even cars *as such*
so fines were not appropriate
anymore than tax bills sent to ghosts

the police and the courts
disagreed

phoned the boss who said it was ok to lend John the money
finished work and walked up to Edward Street with
£200 in a bin bag
the policewoman on the desk surprised
"You must be a good mate"

the cell was tiled high and tiny
John knees up on a bench
swathed in overnight denim fug

we rode
back towards Hove
on top of the bus
this quite a novelty for John
who was more of a car man

peering around in the midmorning Sunday light
a kind of stunned surprise

we shook hands and I never saw him again except
one night in The Greys a curt nod
across a smoky crowd

until last night's dream
still on the journey away from the cell
now with a big car somehow
acquired along the way
stalled at the roadside on the A59 in Lancashire
by the armaments place

so we're on the pavement
knowing the police are on their way and I see
in the back of the vehicle
several sleeping babies – eight soft heads – nestled
in amongst toolboxes and tarpaulins
and I say "Hey, John!
we'll be heroes for rescuing these babies!
This will cancel out all
the fines if only
we explain it properly!
We can spin this!"

An ex-exhibitor dreams about dying in an exhibition centre

The hospital at the NEC was built in less than a fortnight. But since being officially opened by Prince William, it has yet to be put to use. It has a potential capacity to take up to 4,000 patients and is served by a giant mortuary at Birmingham Airport.
- Wolverhampton *Express & Star*, April 26, 2020

we were pioneers of the pop-up scene
arrivers and departers of
shell schemes and space-only stands
rented beneath the roofs of the NEC GMEX Olympia

we spoke from our stations
in temporary frame-towns

then we went away

brands were reinforced
data captured
affinity engaged

we were content before content was king

enduring the effects of white-collar
shore leave in the chromium
bar areas of hotel receptions
sharing drinks with competitor-colleagues
unlikely casual
clothes carried here
from faraway
wardrobes

after a career measured
in footfall it would be a bright and spreading honour
to expire on the exhibition floor
a final small breath under the vast steel roof
then transit
to an airport morgue
on a co-opted monorail

while across the Midlands Plateau lights glint in rows
primordial data shifting
within unseen currents

The Devil's Wall

daily exercise stepping on a plastic cube – a walking journey that goes no distance – tracking device used to monitor heart rate and keep time dutifully displays a map of the route at the conclusion of the exercise period – a small black knot – but zooming in shows a latticework of moves – straight lines making triangles and boxes – a micro choreography autogenerating sigils

while doing this walk of untravelling look out of the window – low curve of horizon – a field leading to the Devil's Wall – built in one night as a pact to steal a human soul – as is often the case the Devil is cheated of the prize – deceived into breaking his own rule by lingering beyond dawn – the trickster tricked and thus a geographical feature formed – see also Devil's Dyke Devil's Elbow Devil's Tower Devil's Arrows Devil's Bridge Devil's Punch Bowl Devil's Chair – diabolical deposits and body parts litter the map

manage about 20 minutes on the stepper plus warmup and cool down – view changes over the months while remaining the same – sense of shifts unseen deep in oceans deep in soil deep in server farms and submarine cables – sense of nowhere to stand but faith in the dawn deliverance

James Bond film 2015

should have seen the way things were going
that time when every cinema ad was
armed men wading through surf whatever
product or service was being promoted.

boundaries – borders – outlines
unspooling
like Mercury snakes in reverse

no message

trackless territory
with little diameter

Things We Did While Alive

had a cleaning job in American Express sudden
view through window by vending machine
pile of roads draping the rise
like a dirty wedding
dress and a delirious (un)true thought: I have been
in every street in this town into every
room

threw away a spindly plastic holder
that provided a handle for the machine
paper beakers of tea/coffee/chocolate

one of the office men stayed behind to ask if I had seen it
which I denied   sudden hot
feeling of guilt   he looked
like a sad horse

lived under pylon lines several
years   scrappy pines dusty reach
towards the long curve of the cables
constant low hum switching
up to a crackling in the wet

power lines a radiant
geometry of loss-prevention
(all the stuff we need is
piped in until it isn't)

walked along the docks   saw five
cardboard coffee beakers impaled
on steel railings like a molecatcher's invoice

James Bond TV premiere 1976

...finally seeing the actual film

the ejectee hurtles from the car
rises a surprisingly short distance
falls and lands
on a grass verge
in front of blocky low-rise night
buildings

guess he walks home
from there

down dissolving time
streets.

Lightning Source UK Ltd.
Milton Keynes UK
UKHW031215220920
370332UK00007B/176